corrugated carton crafting

by
dick van voorst

STERLING
PUBLISHING CO., Inc.   New York
SAUNDERS OF TORONTO, Ltd., Don Mills, Canada

Oak Tree Press Co., Ltd.

London & Sydney

Little Craft Book Series

745.5
V951c

Translated by Eric Greweldinger

Third Printing, 1972
Copyright © 1970 by Sterling Publishing Co., Inc.
419 Park Avenue South, New York, N.Y. 10016
Simultaneously Published and Copyright © 1970 in Canada
by Saunders of Toronto, Ltd., Don Mills, Ontario
British edition published by Oak Tree Press Co., Ltd., Nassau, Bahamas
Distributed in Australia by Oak Tree Press Co., Ltd.,
P.O. Box 34, Brickfield Hill, Sydney 2000, N.S.W.
Distributed in the United Kingdom and elsewhere in the British Commonwealth
by Ward Lock Ltd., 116 Baker Street, London W 1
The original edition was published in The Netherlands under the title
"Golf Karton" © 1968 by Uitgeverij Cantecleer, De Bilt, Holland
Manufactured in the United States of America
All rights reserved
Library of Congress Catalog Card No.: 71–90803
ISBN 0–8069–5138–9   UK 7061–2213–5
5139–7

Contents

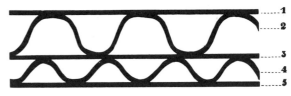

Illus. 1. Double-wall board.

Before You Begin

If you are looking for new materials for handicraft, you will discover that corrugated carton cardboard offers many possibilities. It is a material which can be used to construct decorative objects (such as mobiles, model planes, bridges, machines and homes), or practical objects (like lampshades), as well as many other things. You will find new uses yourself, as the material offers great inspiration and challenge in working with it. An important attraction of corrugated cardboard is that it is easily obtainable, and free. Most of the time, boxes of this beautiful and useful material are discarded as worthless.

This little book offers only a few suggestions for objects and deals with only some techniques—you will create your own objects after developing a "feel" for this material. Feel and imagination will inevitably lead you to a great variety of results. You will see that it is no exaggeration to speak about the almost limitless possibilities of corrugated cardboard!

Types of Board

SINGLE-WALL BOARD (also called double-faced board) consists of two plain cardboard facings, enclosing fluted corrugated cardboard. DOUBLE-WALL BOARD has two sets of flutes with a card board facing in the middle, and a facing on each outside. In Illus. 1 is a cross-section of double-wall board. The layers 1–2–3 and/or 3–4–5, if they were separate, would be called single-wall board.

Where do you get these boards? They can easily be obtained free. Cartons thrown away or delivered by grocery stores or supermarkets are usually single-wall board. Drugstore cartons of small size are, too. Cartons from hardware stores that sell large appliances, such as refrigerators and television sets, are likely to be double-wall board. Both types come from department stores. Since most stores are happy if you take away their used cartons, and the supply is endless, be selective—do not take soiled or damaged boxes, only clean and relatively undamaged ones. Perhaps some day you will convert them into salable cut pieces and strips for craftsmen to use, not only for yourself.

Illus. 2. Plenty of material . . . free!

Tools

A knife or blade in a safe holder, a scissors and a ruler are most important for working with corrugated cartons. The knife blade should be sharp, thin and pointed. The best type for your purpose is one that can be pushed in or out and the front part of the blade broken off when it becomes blunt, so that you can always work with a sharp edge and point. (See Illus. 3.)

Warn children who are too young to handle a knife themselves that they will need help from adults in their cutting.

Scissors are easier for children to use. They are used primarily for cutting "folded" and "bent" strips (Illus. 14 and 15) but can be used in place of a knife blade at times.

You will not need other tools. The only additional things you will need are some adhesive—either a tube of glue, a pot of paste, or a can of rubber cement—and sticks or cane of matchstick size and some cane or dowels, longer but no thicker.

Illus. 3. Various types of knife blades and holders.

Start by Experimenting

Don't try to make an object right away. If you do, you will quickly find that you need experience in every phase of the craft in order to make an airplane, for example, and you will be disappointed with the plane you create. If you start by simply experimenting, you will build up enthusiasm and your mind will become filled with ideas of ways you can cut, strip, peel and glue. In just handling the material and working with it you will discover its possibilities.

Let's try this. Cut one side from a carton of double-wall board and have a good look at the board. You will see that it consists of five layers: two wavelike layers of fluted or corrugated board, which are bonded on each side to flat cardboard facings. Notice that one of the waves is short and the other long—you are going to make use of this fact.

Now look again at Illus. 1—the cross-cut of double-wall board. The layers have been numbered for easy reference. Cut away part of layer #1 (this is easier with some types than with others) and you will expose layer #2, the long wave. If it is difficult to remove layer #1, moisten the board with a sponge and after a short time it will be easy to pull off the top layer.

If you cut a rough circle just in layers #1 and #2, you will make a kind of hole with a flat bottom. If you continue to cut deeper, the hole will go through all five layers. Or you can start cutting another hole through layers #5 and #4 only. You are now ready to start creating an abstract object like a scribble on the wall, which we will call a graffito.

Graffito from a Double-Wall Board

Illus. 4 shows an abstract wall hanging or "picture" made quite easily with one piece of wallboard and a knife. All five different layers of the board were used. You will recognize the long waves of layer #2 and the short waves of layer #4, as well as the plain facings of layers #1, #3 and #5. A knife point was used to cut the shapes, and in places the board was peeled. It is not suggested that you make anything so elaborate as this at the start, especially as it is more difficult to cut curved shapes than straight lines.

Now sketch your own design. For some areas, peel off layer #1, and for other areas and shapes cut off one or more layers at a time. You can vary the depth of cutting while you work, altering and improving your previously made sketch. Surprising effects can be achieved in a composition of varying depths. You can create deep shadows and high planes. Cut the waves cross-wise wherever you can, but also try cutting on a slant.

By exposing the long waves of layer #2 in some places, and the short waves of layer #4 in other places, you will seem to make waves that ripple or go in different directions (as in the middle of Illus. 4).

A double-wall graffito is exciting to create. After trying your hand at some small, rectangular cut-outs on a small board, you can create a larger one. But wait. We will get back to this kind of thing later.

Illus. 4. Graffito cut from double-wall board.

Illus. 5. Cutting a strip
of double-wall board (top view).

How to Cut Strips

Always cut across the waves. You will be surprised how sturdy even $\frac{1}{2}$-inch-wide strips of double-wall board turn out to be.

Illus. 5 and 6 show how to cut strips with a ruler and a blade. Hold the knife at the same angle to the board all the time as you draw the blade along the edge of the ruler. Press with one hand on the ruler to hold it steady as you cut.

If you do not succeed in cutting through all the layers the first time, repeat the process, holding the knife at the same angle. The sharper your knife, the cleaner the cut.

Strips are basic for making the objects described in this book, so practice this experiment until you can cut strips cleanly with one or two strokes.

Illus. 6. Cutting a strip of double-wall board (side view).

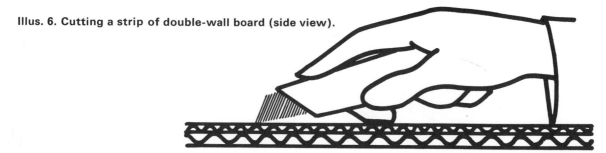

What Can Be Done with Double-Wall Board

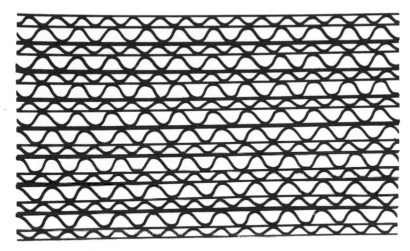

Illus. 7. Stack glued with layer #1 to layer #5 at each level.

Your ½-inch-wide strips can be used straight, bent or folded. Straight strips used for construction are almost always placed in a flat or lying-down position so that the wavelike shape of the corrugation can be seen from the side as in Illus. 1. If you glue such double-wall strips

Illus. 8. Stack glued with layer #1 to #1 and #5 to #5.

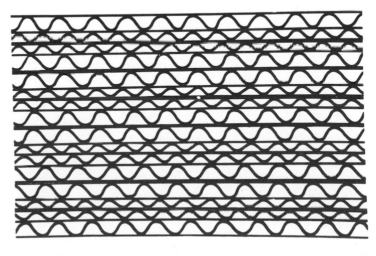

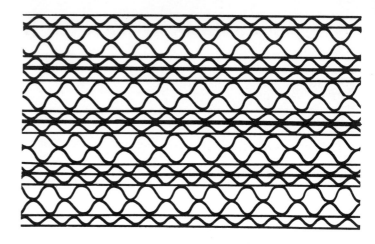

Illus. 9. Stack glued with
layer #2 to #2 and #5 to #5.
Layer #1 has been peeled off.

together in regular fashion you can obtain a beautiful, open-work type of design (Illus. 7 and 8).

If, instead, you first peel off layer #1 and attach layer #2 (as labelled in Illus. 1) to layer #2, and layer #5 to layer #5, you will make some bigger waves in between the layers (Illus. 9).

Now you can vary this still more by removing with your blade some of the short waves and layers #3 and #5 at intervals, such as at every second or third large wave (Illus. 10).

Illus. 10. Stack glued as in Illus. 9 with some areas cut away.

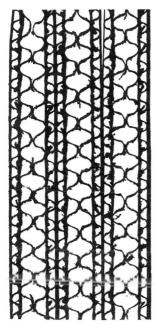

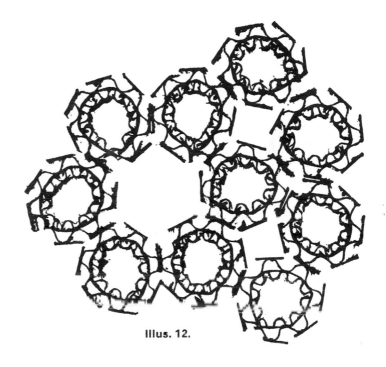

Illus. 12.

Illus. 11.

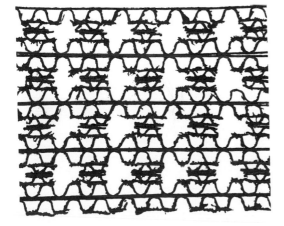

You will discover for yourself how to make many other nice open-work patterns. Just a few further suggestions are shown in Illus. 11, 12 and 13.

Illus. 13.

Bending

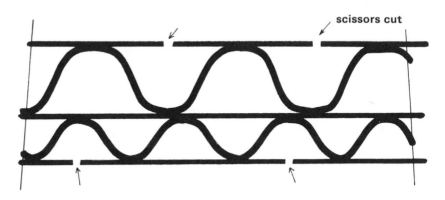

scissors cut

Illus. 14. Each long wave has been cut, but only alternating short waves.

Start with straight strips, either $\frac{1}{2}$ inch wide or wider. You will "bend" these, not by rolling the board but by making incisions with your scissors at certain points. You can make these cuts in layer #1 in between each of the large waves, and also in layer #5 but only in alternate waves (Illus. 14). You can then bend the strip easily. You can vary this by making incisions at every wave in both layers which will allow an even sharper bend (Illus. 15).

You can even bend without scissor cuts. Just remove layers #1 and #5, and you will have a very pliable strip that will coil like a snake (Illus. 16).

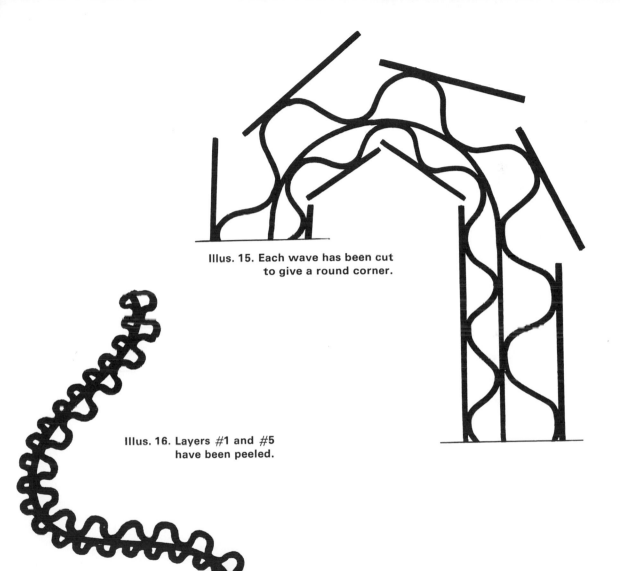

Illus. 15. Each wave has been cut to give a round corner.

Illus. 16. Layers #1 and #5 have been peeled.

15

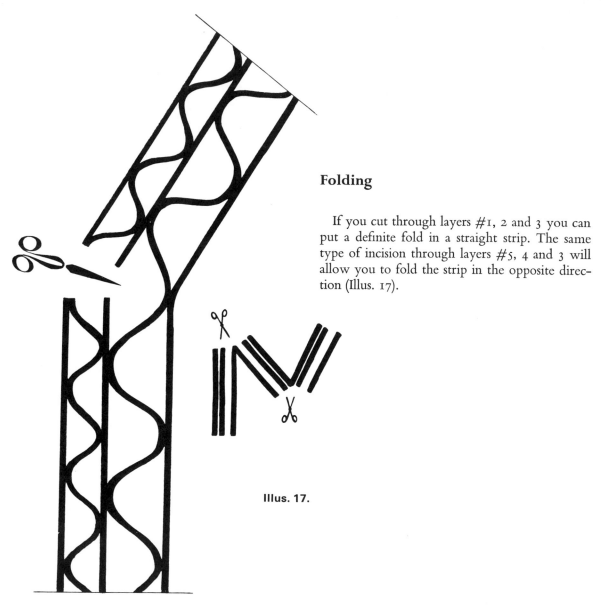

Folding

If you cut through layers #1, 2 and 3 you can put a definite fold in a straight strip. The same type of incision through layers #5, 4 and 3 will allow you to fold the strip in the opposite direction (Illus. 17).

Illus. 17.

Building a Straight-Strip House

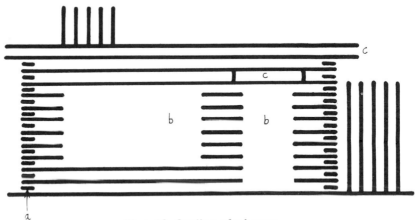

Illus. 18. Outline of a house.

Now that you have made various types of strips, you are ready to start using them. Choose a house first, any type. The descriptions and illustrations of houses here are meant only to acquaint you with the technique. The design is up to you.

For a start, try a house like the one in Illus. 18. The walls (a) are ½-inch-wide strips glued in a regular pattern with waves dove-tailed at the corners. For windows and doors you merely leave out strips (b), or cut out parts of strips.

The roof and awning (c) are a little more complicated. They are made from a piece of corrugated board cut in a rectangle. There are two possible variations:

1. Make horizontal and vertical incisions in layer #1 of your rectangular piece of board, so that you have a checkerboard pattern. Then pull off every other square (Illus. 19).

2. Use only layers #1 and #2 of a single-wall board and make parallel lines cross-wise over the waves (crushing them) at distances of an inch or an inch and a half apart. You can make the lines with either the flat side of a knife blade or with the closed points of a scissors. The crushed waves will produce a zigzag pattern.

The assembling of the parts is left to you. Just be sure you have a stable base. Illus. 20 shows you how one house was constructed of straight strips.

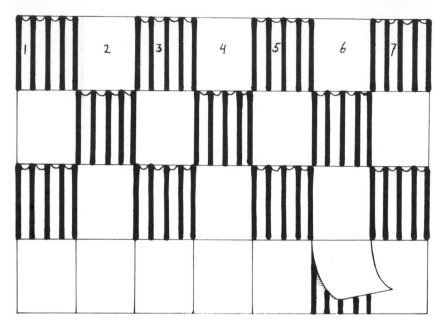

Illus. 19. Outline of a roof.

Illus. 20. House made of single-wall board, the chimney of double-wall board. The inside of an old light-bulb was used for the television aerial.

Building with Straight and Bent Strips

If you are not limited to straight strips, you can make round forms for doors, for example (as in Illus. 21), by using bent strips. When laid flat, this type of strip is "transparent." (You will be able to see through the holes.)

Illus. 21. House made of straight and bent strips.

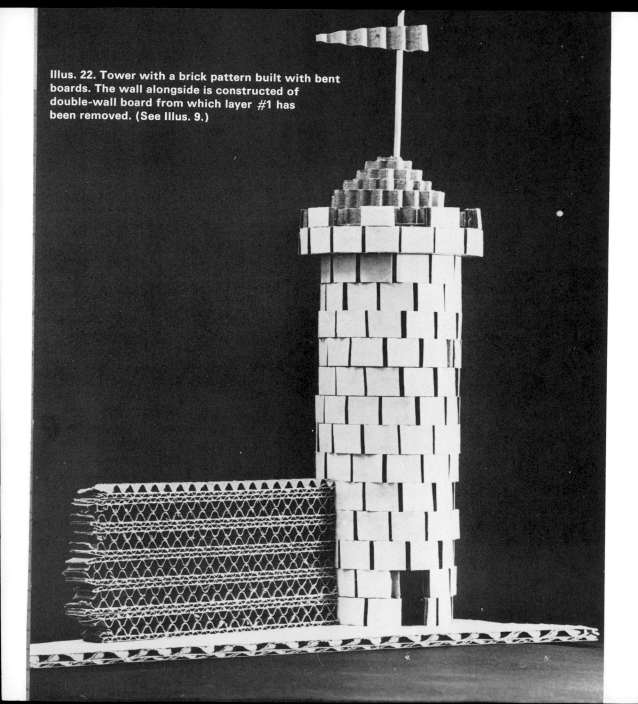

Illus. 22. Tower with a brick pattern built with bent boards. The wall alongside is constructed of double-wall board from which layer #1 has been removed. (See Illus. 9.)

To make columns, towers and castles that are not transparent, in other words, round objects that look solid, you must use bent strips and glue them together at their edges instead of flat (as in

Illus. 23. Brick pattern non-transparent tower.

Illus. 24. Cone made of strips.

the tower in Illus. 22). Small gaps will appear where you have made your incisions but that does not spoil the solid look.

To minimize the gaps, you can plan a brick design (Illus. 23 and 25). Put strips of equal length together so that the gaps (as in brickwork) are in shifted positions on each line.

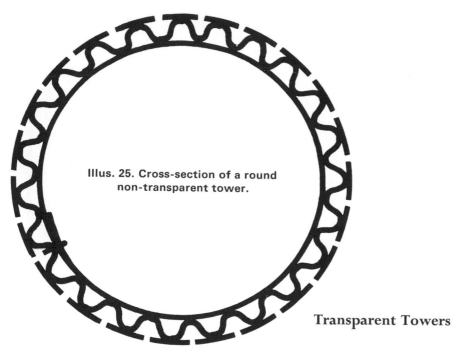

Illus. 25. Cross-section of a round non-transparent tower.

A simple tower can be made by glueing bent strips around a cylinder armature, such as a toilet tissue roll. Without an armature you can construct a cone (as in Illus. 24) by glueing strips of decreasing length together. Start with a wide base, then building up, glue on three strips a little narrower, then three more still narrower, etc., until you reach a peak, where you can insert a flag or banner.

Transparent Towers

Straight strips without incisions will give you a transparent effect when used vertically, edge out. To make a transparent tower, cut a number of strips of equal width (*a* in Illus. 26), and stack them together. Before you stand them on end, cut two or more strips of thick paper (wrapping paper will do) and glue these paper strips (*b* in Illus. 26) at the top and bottom of one side of the stack of cardboard strips, leaving a paper tab of about an inch. If you want more reinforcement for a tall tower, glue a strip across at the middle too. Now bend the construction into a round shape with the paper strips inside. Glue the tabs of the paper strips to the inside of the opposite end. Your tower will stand round and straight, and you will be able to see through it.

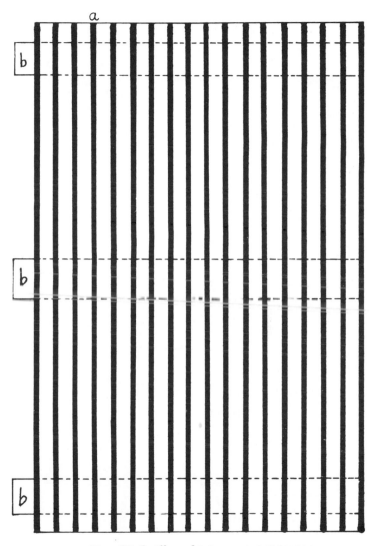

Illus. 26. Outline of a transparent tower.

Using Sticks for Strength

Up until now, you have been using corrugated board alone. But you can reinforce it with little sticks of cane or even wooden matchsticks (with the heads burned off). Place the sticks in the holes created by the waves of the corrugation. With this added strength, you will have construction material similar to wood, but you can still cut the pieces to size with your blade as the wood is soft and thin.

A Watchtower

First make the house, more or less as you did before (see Illus. 27 and 28). Glue the roof, window and awning on to the house. Then to

Illus. 27. Outline of a watchtower: *a* is the base, *b* the stilts, *c* a folded joint, *d* the house, and *e* a ladder with cane steps.

Illus. 28. A different watchtower, jointed with sticks of cane.

make the stilts, cut a number of strips of equal length, and make sure they have the same number of waves. The more accurately you work, the more stable your tower will be.

Take your square or rectangular base (*a* in Illus. 27) and either set the feet of the stilts on top of it, or set it on the feet (as in Illus. 28) so that you get a firm foundation. You can attach the base and the feet together by putting sticks that are long enough between the waves of the two parts or by glueing them together.

You are now ready to erect the diagonals which form triangles, giving rigidity to the structure. They can be simple, as in Illus. 27, or complex, as in Illus. 28. The important thing is that they lock into the house and stand firmly on the base and feet. You can use a folded joint (as in *c* in Illus. 27.) Here again, the sticks are handy

for reinforcing the joints and need only be set between the waves of the stilts and the waves of the horizontal pieces.

For a ladder, cut a strip and insert lengths of wood through every other wave, letting it stick out on each side.

A Bridge

The road surface of the bridge should be smooth, so use a single-wall strip about 18 inches long and at least 5 inches wide, and set it on piers (*f* in Illus. 29). The piers can be boxes or just squares of board glued or joined together with sticks. Just be sure the piers are equal in height so that the bridge is level.

For arches, cut straight strips of equal length,

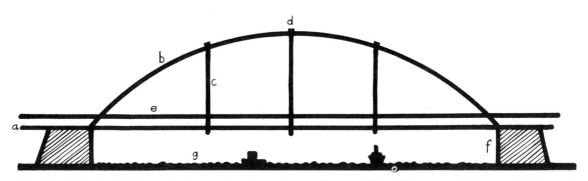

Illus. 29. A simple bridge: *a* is the road surface, *b* an arch, *c* a cable, *d* the central joint, *e* a horizontal support, *f* a pier, and *g* the waves below.

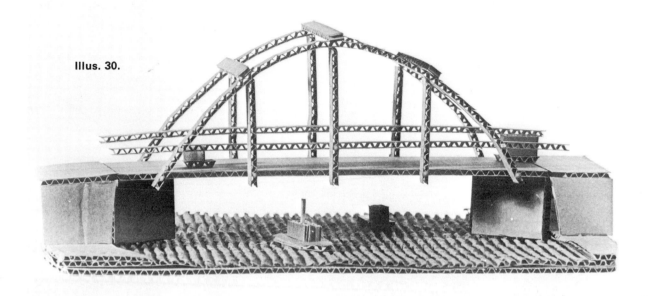

Illus. 30.

at least $1\frac{1}{2}$ times as long as the road strip. Bend these strips by making incisions as before, and attach the arched strips (*b* in Illus. 29) to the sides of the road surface with sticks through the waves. The ends of the arches can pass a little below the surface (see Illus. 30).

The cables that connect the arch with the surface (*c* in Illus. 29) are thin strips. Set the middle one first and join it with a stick at the arch (at *d*), and at the roadway. Then put other cables along the arch, as many as you want, but space them evenly.

In Illus. 30, you will see beams that reinforce

the arches and cables, and hold the whole bridge together. The struts across the tops of the arches are glued, and the long horizontal supports are attached with sticks.

The water is easily represented, as we work with waves! Just peel off the facing layer of a single-wall board. Boats go on the water, and cars on the bridge. Illus. 30 suggests some of the river and road traffic. Use your imagination and create your own.

Your bridge can be low, like these, or high above the water, long or short, and can even be a drawbridge.

Illus. 31. Church of open-work construction. Note the bent bell.

Illus. 32. A biplane made by a 16-year-old boy. It measures about 20 inches long by 20 inches wide. Made of strips, it is held together with sticks. (Note the struts and tail assembly.)

Building Things that Move

In making things that move, you will be fascinated, and once you start you will find it difficult to stop. You will continue to be amazed by the possibilities.

Mobile objects are mainly composed of strips. Instead of nuts and bolts, however, sticks or struts of cane or wood are used. It is even more important, when you have moving parts, that you cut and build precisely. Count the holes carefully, because two strips that are equal in length may not match up exactly when you go to place a stick between them.

With moving objects, you want to build them so that they can be set in motion simply by the downward movement of your hand. Rather than describe these mechanisms in words, let us examine the diagrams of two: Illus. 33 and 34. The main thrill will come from building a mechanism that you have invented yourself.

Illus. 33 is a simple mechanism and Illus. 34 a complicated one. Start with the simple. The base is a piece of single- or double-wall board that cannot warp. The fixed strips (*a*) are double-wall and reinforced by a cross-bar (*b*). Each moving

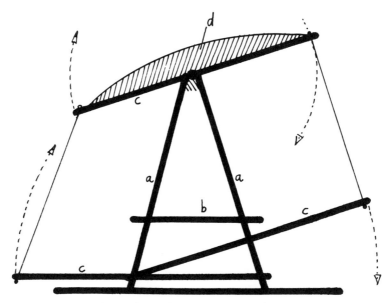

Illus. 33. A simple mechanism.

strip (labelled *c*) is attached with a stick acting as a joint to a fixed strip. Check this in the diagram.

Each moving strip is also connected by means of a piece of string directly to another strip that moves. The top *c* is like a seesaw. As it tilts up on the right, it goes down on the left; lower right *c* rises as upper right *c* goes up, and vice versa.

The top of the seesaw may be reinforced with a second strip glued at a right angle down the length of it (see Illus. 35). The top beam thus will be in the shape of a T when viewed from the end.

All this seems to be more complicated than it really is. If you start, you will see how the pieces go together.

Illus. 34. A more complicated mechanism.

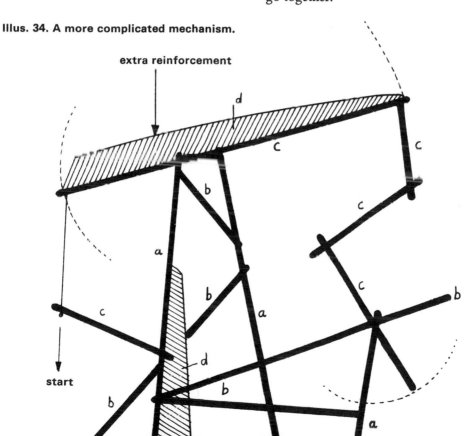

extra reinforcement

start

Illus. 34 also follows elementary engineering principles. The shaded areas marked *d* are extra strips again glued at right angles as reinforcement to the main strip. All moving parts are labelled *c*. You will note that when the lower left *c* drops down it pulls top left *c* down and sends top right *c* up. This forces the wings of lower right *c* to straighten out. All parts labelled *a* are fixed strips and those labelled *b* are reinforcement strips. Sewing thread or nylon fishing line, which is strong yet thin, is best.

Illus. 35 in a close-up shows you how the sticks are set into the double-wall strips.

Do not make the exact objects illustrated here—create your own.

(Opposite page)

Illus. 35. Construction with sticks as joints for moving parts. The boy is putting the stick through a wave and will move the whole strip down to fasten it into a vertical upright strip.

Building Mechanisms with Wheels

Here you will need solid wheels made of strips from which layer #1 has been peeled. After peeling a long strip, roll it with the wave side out into a tight coil. For the mechanism in Illus. 36, you will need a 2-inch-wide strip about 10 inches long. Fix the end of the coil well with adhesive on the smooth side.

Through the middle of this wheel you now put an axle of cane or wood, about as long as a lollipop stick. Make another wheel or two in the same fashion. By attaching two wheels together with a loop of single-wall peeled strip, and setting the mechanism on a super-structure, you will have a motor. Flick a wheel and it will set the motor in motion.

How to continue is a matter of your own inventiveness. The diagrams here (Illus. 36, 37, 38) give you only some of many possibilities. Illus. 36 shows how the waves of the loop fit perfectly into the waves of the wheel.

Illus. 37 is another view of a wheel assembly, such as is used in Illus. 36.

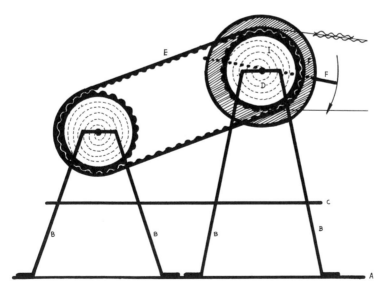

Illus. 36. Side view of a mechanism with wheels and endless belt.

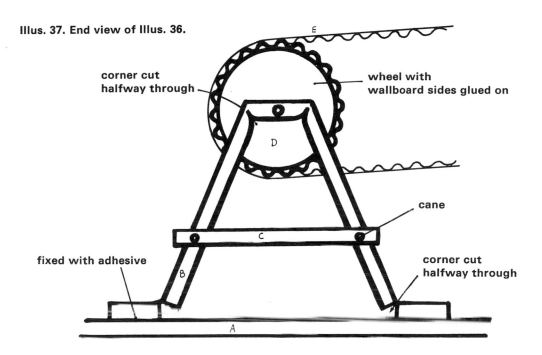

Illus. 37. End view of Illus. 36.

corner cut
halfway through

wheel with
wallboard sides glued on

E

D

cane

fixed with adhesive

corner cut
halfway through

B

C

A

Working with Wide Strips

You used a strip 2 inches wide in making the wheels for Illus. 36. These wider strips used for the mechanism with wheels offer new possibilities. You can make objects of greater sturdiness than with ½-inch-wide strips.

To make the mechanism in Illus. 36, start as usual with a strong double-thick wallboard base (A). On this, set the supports (B) to carry the wheels. Illus. 37 is a close-up side view of the assembly while Illus. 38 is a detailed end view. These show you where to cut and bend the supports and how the cane or sticks are used as axles and fasteners.

To be able to turn the wheel (D), which you can cover with wallboard sides to make it look neater, push a cane or little round stick through the middle as an axle. This axle must protrude far enough out on each side to be placed in the supports (see Illus. 38). You may want to use an extra long stick that will extend well beyond one of the supports so that you can attach a second wheel for turning the mechanism.

The wheel can be turned at F (Illus. 36) just by using your forefinger or you can simply twist the axle with your fingers.

Do you get the idea? When you have the ability to make wheels turn, your mind starts turning over possibilities too.

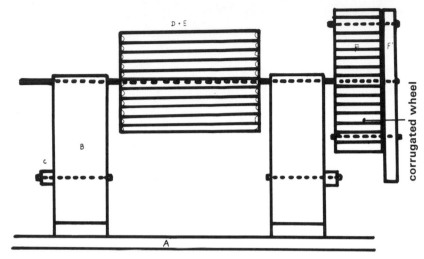

corrugated wheel

Illus. 38. Close-up of side view of wheel in Illus. 36.

Movements

What will your mechanism do? That is the main question children ask. Motion is one thing, and function is another. You may now have to invent some work for the machine. From the craftsman's point of view, however, working with the material is the important thing.

If you have an idea of how to use another wheel, go ahead and set one up. The fun really starts when you have a whole series of wheels joined by belts or loops.

For a continuous belt, take a single-wall narrow strip, as before, and peel it off layer #1. When you have arranged it properly and tightly over your wheels, glue the ends together. Then by turning one of your wheels you can run the belt over the tops, backward and forward, setting all your wheels in motion.

You might introduce flaps that open and close, or make a set-up that has a wheel in between supports, or make a strip that tips upward or downward in unexpected ways. Don't give up if your contraption does not work as expected, but start again and adapt what you started, making it work in a different way. There is no hard and fast rule that you have to follow, except the general rules of physics. Incidentally, if a youngster is working on these projects, he will learn a number of physical principles.

Illus. 39. A complicated contraption
with wheels and belts joined with cane.

Creating Designs with Boards and Strips

From practical science to abstract art is but a short step. Illus. 40 and 41 show two examples of free-flowing designs cut from wallboard. How do you cut them?

Cutting at an Oblique Angle

Until now you have cut mostly cross-wise to the waves, or along their length. Now you have to cut diagonally and with rounded lines. Use the point of your knife and cut so that the waves are left clean, not ragged. You can either draw a pencil line on your wallboard before cutting, or cut freehand, depending on your art ability. You may also want to cut a groove or track of double lines through the top layer and peel off the track.

Illus. 40 shows how shapes have been cut from wallboard and extracted, leaving the waves exposed in the cut-away areas. A grooved track down the middle tends to hold the abstract together.

Illus. 41 looks like a jigsaw cutting, but the pieces cannot be removed. The lines represent a cutting with the knife point, single or double track. Single-track cutting will simply leave an indentation or groove in the surface, while with double-track you can peel away the top layer and expose the waves.

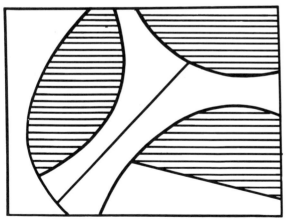

Illus. 40. Shapes that can be cut out of wallboard with a knife.

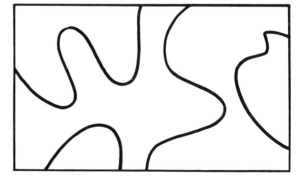

Illus. 41. These shapes can be grooved but they cannot be cut out and removed.

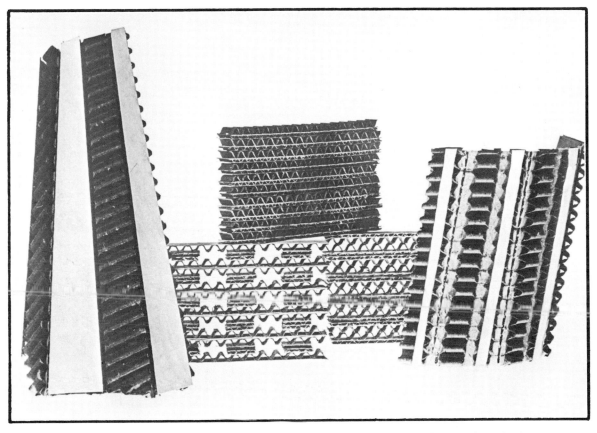

Illus. 42. You can build an abstract city with angled stacks that cast interesting shadows.

Angled Stacks

As you see in Illus. 42, you can create some interesting stacks, transparent and solid, tilting left or right, looking like pyramids or like blocks. When you place them for exhibition, try to get the light to cast shadows to add further texture. Leaving your open-work blocks in the background provides a feeling of lightness to any arrangement.

Cane as a Main Element

Previously you used wood and cane in a subordinate way, simply to assist you in construction. Now use it for your main construction, with wallboard to add shape, as in Illus. 43.

You will need strips of cane of various lengths and thicknesses, or wooden dowels if you cannot get cane easily. You will also need a steel ruler.

In this work, imagination is more important than technical ability, for you can build anything you want. Take the modern ship design in Illus. 43 as a start. The ship's hull is double-thick board. Cane was stuck through the wave holes to secure it to the base, and also to set the sails and the top of the mast. Extra bundles of the sticks, stuck through the wave holes, provide an angled line to indicate forward movement.

Illus. 43. Sailing ship such as has never been seen before.

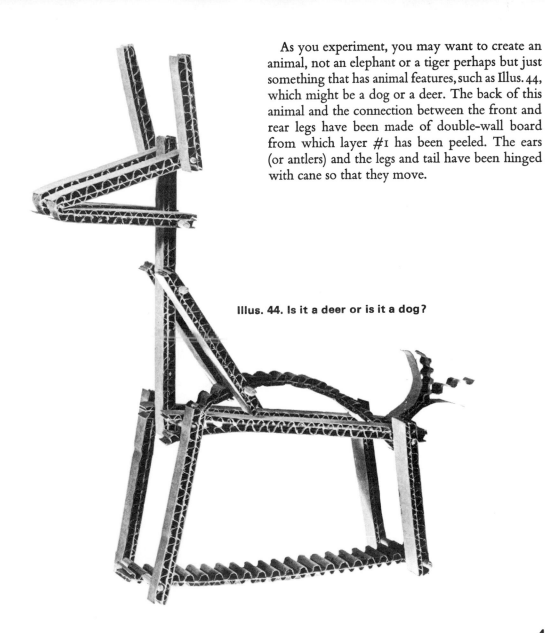

As you experiment, you may want to create an animal, not an elephant or a tiger perhaps but just something that has animal features, such as Illus. 44, which might be a dog or a deer. The back of this animal and the connection between the front and rear legs have been made of double-wall board from which layer #1 has been peeled. The ears (or antlers) and the legs and tail have been hinged with cane so that they move.

Illus. 44. Is it a deer or is it a dog?

Making a Lampshade

First cut a sheet of drawing paper to the size you want your lampshade to be when laid out flat, allowing about $\frac{1}{2}$ inch overlap for the tab which will serve as the binding strip and be glued down. Paste this pattern down on the single- or double-wall board stock that you want to use. Adjust your pattern so that you will be cutting straight across the waves.

Then cut out the wallboard with your blade, leaving the drawing paper pasted on. You can now peel off the drawing paper and layer #1 with it, leaving the waves on the outside. Roll the shade now to the circumference you want and glue the tab that you have left. You can bend the tab back and have the tab waves lock into parallel waves, or the waves can be glued to the inside layer. (See Illus. 45.)

To keep the lampshade's round shape you need a disc or circle to set in the top, or to fit the bottom, or both. You can use wallboard for these discs (or plywood if you prefer). As shown in Illus. 46, cut two circles of the same diameter, and with a radius equal to approximately one-sixth of the circumference. The central hole in (a) is for the lamp's finial to go through, and the free-form holes are to allow the lamp's heat to go out, as well as to create interesting spotted effects on the ceiling. The rim (b) should be grooved so that the edge of the shade will fit into it. Glue the rim to the shade.

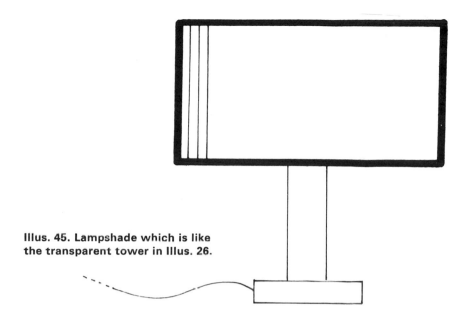

Illus. 45. Lampshade which is like the transparent tower in Illus. 26.

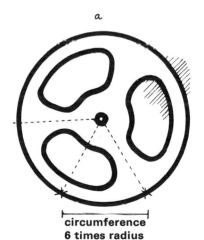

circumference
6 times radius

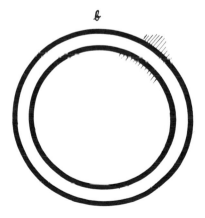

Illus. 46. Top of lampshade (*a*) and bottom (*b*).

Making Mobiles

What is a mobile? An object or combination of objects attached by string or wire to the ceiling or any high place and floating freely in space as the currents of air move it. Because a mobile needs to be light, corrugated board is an ideal material.

The possibilities are almost endless. You can use strips of wallboard and $\frac{1}{2}$-inch-wide wheels, for example, as in Illus. 47.

The wheels are made as before by bending (see Illus. 14 and 15) the $\frac{1}{2}$-inch-wide strips. You can roll your wheels tightly, but for this purpose it is better to roll them loosely instead, allowing the many small holes to show. You may want to glue colored transparent paper to some of the wheels. Another alternative is to attach a second wheel to the first with adhesive tape.

You will discover very quickly how to balance your wheel mobile when you hang the wheels with string to corrugated board strips (see Illus. 47).

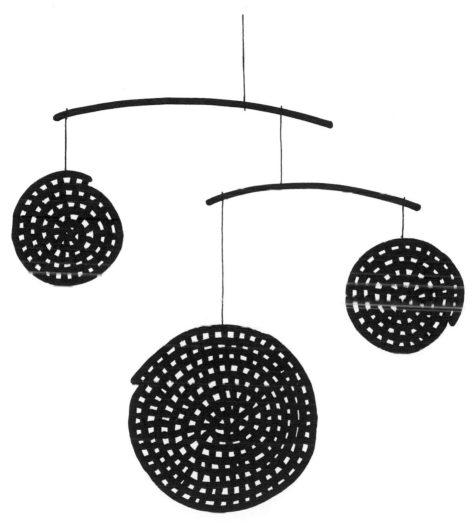

Illus. 47. Mobile.

Illus. 48. Stork and marsh grass made
of strips glued to drawing paper.
Some strips are peeled, others
bent by the incision method.

Drawing with Wallboard and Light

Cut a number of strips of single-wall board ½-inch wide and 20 inches long, and peel off one layer. Then take a large sheet of drawing paper (for instance, 30 by 40 inches) and sketch your drawing on it. You may then want to make the paper transparent, and you can do this by coating it with paraffin or turpentine.

Following your layout, glue the corrugated strips to the paper with the wave side perpendicular to the paper. (You can glue the smooth layer side down if you want, but glueing the side of the cut to the paper is preferred.)

The stork in Illus 48 was made of strips from which layer #1 had been peeled in some cases, and left on in other cases, with incisions made in the strips where bending was needed.

If you place such a wallboard "drawing" in a window (especially if it has been made transparent) light will illuminate it from behind and filter through, giving it a very artistic effect.

You might consider building a frame of wallboard around your drawing, and hanging it on the wall. In this case it might be best to build the drawing on wallboard to start with, instead of on drawing paper, depending on the size, of course.

By now you have worked enough with corrugated boards so that you need no further instruction. Just let your imagination run free and your fingers do the work.

Index

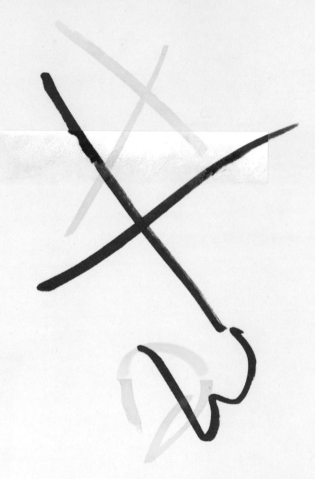